A Tribute to
THE YOUNG AT HEART

R.L. STINE

By Jill C. Wheeler

Published by Abdo & Daughters, 4940 Viking Drive, Suite 622, Edina, Minnesota 55435.

Library bound edition distributed by Rockbottom Books, Pentagon Tower, P.O. Box 36036, Minneapolis, Minnesota 55435.

Cover Photo credit: Frank Veronsky
Interior Photo credits: Archive Photos, pages 13, 15
Frank Veronsky 23
Publishers Weekly 5

Edited by Julie Berg

Library of Congress cataloging-in-Publication

Wheeler, Jill C., 1964—
    R.L. Stine / Jill C. Wheeler.
    p.   cm. -- (The Young at Heart)
    Includes index.
    Summary: Biography of the American author who likes to have kids
turn to reading for entertainment. Who keeps his books funny, and who loves to scare
others through his reading.

    ISBN 1-56239-521-1
    1. Stine, R. L. --Biography--juvenile literature. 2 Authors, American-
-20th century--biography--juvenile literature. 3. Childrens stories--authorship--juvenile
literature. [1. Stine, R. L. 2. Authors, American.] I. Title. II. Series: Tribute to the
Young at Heart.
    PS3569.T4837Z97   1996
    813'.54--dc20   95-41217
    [B]   CIP
                                              AC

TABLE OF CONTENTS

GIVE ME GOOSEBUMPS!

Todd Barstow loved worms. He had a worm farm in his basement. He scared his sister and her friends with worms. He put them in their hair. He slid them down their backs.

One day, Todd cut a worm in half. Suddenly, he saw the other worms staring at him. Soon, worms started showing up everywhere. They were in his bed and clothes. They popped up in his sandwich. They tumbled out of the faucet as he took a bath. Fat, brown and purple worms trapped Todd in the tub!

Finally, a giant worm crawled out of the ground and began to strangle him ...

So goes the story in *Go Eat Worms* by R. L. Stine. Stine is the bestselling author of the "Goosebumps" and "Fear Street" horror book series for young people.

R. L. Stine is the bestselling author of the "Goosebumps" series.

Stine enjoyed ghost stories when he was young, just like his readers do now. When he was little, many people listened to radio programs. Some were scary shows, like *The Shadow* and *Suspense*. Stine recalls listening to those shows, too. "I remember being real scared, lying in bed listening to these scary things on the radio. I loved that."

As he got older, Stine also read science-fiction books and joke books. He shared them with his classmates and made them laugh. Later, he put his stories together in little magazines and shared them with his friends. "I loved writing and typing these stories," he said.

Stine continued to write in college. He studied English at Ohio State University. Between classes, he edited the school's humor magazine. "That's mainly what I did at Ohio State," he said. "I'd hang out at the magazine office and put out this magazine every month."

R. L. Stine enjoyed reading ghost stories when he was young.

The job also gave him a dream. "I loved magazines and wanted to get some kind of magazine job. My ambition in life was to someday be editor of my own humor magazine." He graduated from Ohio State in 1965.

Stine taught social studies at a junior high school in Columbus for one year. Then he decided to do something else with his life. In 1966, he packed his bags and headed for New York City.

MAGAZINES AND MAKE-BELIEVE

In New York, Stine worked at a fan magazine. He made-up interviews with famous people. "The editor would come by in the morning and say, 'Do an interview with the Beatles.' So I'd make-up an interview with the Beatles."

"It was great training," he added. "In a way it was very creative work. We had to make-up everything. Sometimes we would do the same story two different ways."

After the fan magazine, Stine worked for another magazine called *Soft Drink Industry*. People who made and sold soft drinks read it. Stine hated the work. But he learned to write fast. "I would have to do 20 articles a day from stacks of news clippings on my desk," he said. "It taught me not to stop and think about it. I just had to sit down and write."

In 1968, Stine became an assistant editor for *Junior Scholastic Magazine*. Finally, he had found a job he enjoyed. He also met Jane Waldorn at the magazine. The two got married on June 22, 1969.

Stine stayed with *Junior Scholastic Magazine* for four years. He then became editor of a brand new social studies magazine called *Search*.

Stine's dream came true in 1975. He edited a new humor magazine for children called *Bananas*. "I was doing what I had always wanted to do." He was only 32 years old.

TV3950   seventeen

BANANAS

CHERYL LADD
The Human Angel

R. L. Stine was the editor of a children's
humor magazine called *Bananas*.

HOW TO BE FUNNY

Bananas was popular with children twelve years and older. It was produced by the same company that published the humor magazine *Hot dog!* Some adults were reading it, too. One was a publishing company editor. She asked Stine to write a children's book. He had never thought about doing that before. He thought it over. Then he told her he would come up with an idea.

How To Be Funny was Stine's first humorous children's book. It landed in bookstores in 1982. "It was how to be funny in the cafeteria, at the breakfast table, in bed at night," he said. It was the kind of book parents hated.

How To Be Funny also started Stine on a new career path. He began to write many funny books. For some, he wrote under the name Jovial Bob Stine. His wife helped him write some books, too. He also wrote books under the name R.L. Stine that let readers come up with their own plot. These books offered different twists and endings. Readers could choose the ending they liked best.

Hot dog! was produced by the same company that published *Bananas.*

Meanwhile, Stine continued to edit *Bananas*. However, young people were losing interest in the magazine. Stine's publisher decided to replace *Bananas* in 1984. The company made Stine editor of another magazine called *Maniac*.

Scholastic published *Maniac* for just one year. In 1985, the company reorganized. Stine lost his job. But he didn't worry. "I was already doing all kinds of books for children for different publishers, so I came home and started writing more books."

Stine stayed in touch with his friends at Scholastic. One worked on "The Baby-Sitters Club" series. She asked him to write a scary novel for young adults. The friend gave him the title of the book — *Blind Date*. Stine had to write a novel that fit the title. He did. *Blind Date* came out in 1986. It sold many copies. Now, Stine was a novelist.

SPOOKY SUCCESS

Stine had stumbled onto an exciting new market. Publishers found that young people loved to be scared. Stine was happy to scare them. He wrote *Twisted* in 1986. In 1989, he wrote *The Baby-sitter*, the story of how a young girl's after-school job turns frightening. It is one of Stine's most popular books.

Stine recalled his own childhood and what scared him. Then he wrote about scary people and of heroes and heroines in danger. His books became more and more popular. Suddenly, he forgot about writing funny stories.

One day, Stine and his wife had an idea. His wife had her own publishing company. She called it Parachute Press. They decided young readers might like a series of scary stories that came out every other month.

Now it was time to work on a series concept. "I sat down and thought," Stine said. "I needed a good title, then I could figure out a way to do a series of scary books.

R. L. Stine wrote the "Fear Street" and "Goosebumps" series.

When the words 'Fear Street' sort of magically appeared, I wrote it down, then came up with the concept."

Stine imagined what "Fear Street" would be like. It would be a place where terrible, frightening things happened. Scary legends and spooky events would fill the street which would link all the books in the series.

Jane took the idea to a publisher. They agreed to give it a try.

WELCOME TO "FEAR STREET"

Stine signed a six-book "Fear Street" contract. His first book was *The New Girl* in 1989. In it, the main character wonders whether or not his new girlfriend really exists. Of course, she lives on Fear Street.

The "Fear Street" series is very popular among nine-to fourteen-year-olds. Stine is still adding titles. There are more than 30 "Fear Street" books today. Stine has even made different groups within the series. There's the "Fear Street: Super Chiller" series, the "Fear Street Saga" series, the "Ghosts of Fear Street" books, and the "Fear Street Cheerleaders" series. There are new cheerleaders on Fear Street every year because so many die.

Stine also writes horror for younger readers. His famous "Goosebumps" series began in 1982. "Goosebumps" books are for children ages eight to twelve.

The books feature many plot twists and cliff-hanger chapter endings, which his readers enjoy.

"Children like to be scared," he said. "They like the fact that there is some kind of jolt at the end of every chapter. They know that if they read to the end of the chapter they're going to have some kind of funny surprise."

The surprises aren't fatal, however. No one in "Goosebumps" ever dies. Stine wants kids to feel safe reading his books. "Part of the appeal is that they're safe scares," he said. "You're home in your room and reading. The books are not half as scary as the real world."

There are now more than 30 "Goosebumps" titles. Stine also has written "Goosebumps" books that let readers create the plots. The "Give Yourself Goosebumps" series lets readers pick from 20 different scary endings.

"They kind of make you curious," said one young reader. "You don't want to stop reading."

SCARING-UP INSPIRATION

Stine patterns his characters after real teenagers. "I spend a lot of time with my son Matthew and his friends," he said. "I spy on them, listen to their music, see how they dress." Stine's research pays off. His characters sound and dress like real people. Sometimes, Stine uses Matthew's antics in his stories. He also takes character names from Matthew's school directory.

Matthew is a teenager. He hasn't read most of his father's books. "I'm insulted by that," Stine said. "But that's why he does it, of course."

Stine also likes to spice up his books with "cheap thrills." He describes them as "disgusting, gross things to put in the book. Like the cat is boiled in the spaghetti, a girl pours honey over a boy and sets ants on him," he said. His readers love that. He has several other keys to writing for kids.

R. L. Stine with his wife and son at home in New York City.

"For one thing, the plots have to be logical," he said. "If they get too scary, they get silly, and nobody will believe it. But if they're too believable, then they'll be boring. The hard thing is to make them scary without going over that edge. You have to remember what scared you as a kid."

His publisher said Stine has done just that. "People have tried to imitate his work, but it's not easily done. Bob (Stine) really understands kids."

"Somebody once called me the Jekyll and Hyde of children's publishing," Stine added. "For a long time I mainly wrote humor for kids. Now I don't do funny stuff anymore. Now I'm scary all the time."

A PICTURE'S WORTH A THOUSAND CHILLS

Stine doesn't find it hard to write two books a month. He can write about 20 pages a day. He works six days a week. His office is in a bedroom of his Manhattan apartment. He and his family have lived there for more than 20 years. "I've never had a day when I couldn't sit down and just write," he said.

"I start with a picture. *Stay Out of the Basement* began with the image of a father taking off his baseball cap. He has leaves instead of hair curling out of his head. *The Horror at Camp Jellyjam* started with an image of a huge blobby creature sweating snails. They were just popping out of his body constantly. For *Go Eat Worms*, I pictured a boy taking a bath. Worms came out of the faucet and crawled down the walls."

"So far, when I say I need an idea, I get one," he added. "Thank God, since I have to produce two books a month. One of these days I'll just sit there, and it'll be all over. But I never panic."

Sometimes Stine cannot believe his success. In April 1994, he returned to his hometown of Columbus, Ohio, to do a book signing. He was driving to the store when he ran into a traffic jam. The traffic was so bad the police had to be called.

"I thought there had been an accident," Stine said. "Until I realized the cars were all filled with kids. They were coming to see me." That evening about 1,000 fans showed up. He signed autographs for five hours. He no longer does book signings. "This may sound horrible, but too many kids come," he said. "It's just not fair to keep them waiting so long."

"The money is beyond my wildest dreams," he added. "I don't know what to do with it. Really. How many times can I send Matt to college?

"I'm not competent at anything else, but I'm good at this," he added. "It's what I always wanted to do." When he's not writing, Stine likes to swim, read, and watch old movies from the 1930s and 1940s.

HOOKING YOUNG PEOPLE ON BOOKS

Stine feels good about what he writes. "It's important that kids should be able to discover they can turn to reading for entertainment instead of television or Nintendo," he said. His books avoid drugs or abuse. He wants to keep them fun.

Many adults applaud Stine for his work. "I just think it's a safe way to be scared," said another author. "If you're scared by a book, you can close it. You have control over the situation. So on the one hand, it's a controlling-your-fear kind of thing."

A children's bookstore owner agrees. "I've had parents come in here who say, 'My kids never read a book, and now they do.' Stine is a hero to these kids." Many bookstores are very busy around the first of the month. That's when the new books come out. Local bookstores save copies of each new Stine book for some of their young readers.

Stine receives an average of 400 fan letters a day. One said, "I hate to read but I love your books." Another said, "I never read any books because I don't like to read. But I buy every book you write."

Some readers entered a special contest. They wrote essays on what scares them. The contest winners had their pictures "monsterized." Artists changed their pictures. They looked like they had just read a "Goosebumps" book and were frightened.

"It's rewarding for me," Stine said. "I feel so lucky that these books have become so popular."

GLOSSARY

Antics — funny activities.

Autograph — a person's signature, written by hand.

Characters — the people in novels or plays.

Concept — an idea.

Interview — when a writer asks someone questions to learn about them.

Jekyll and Hyde — characters in a famous scary novel. Dr. Jekyll drinks a potion and turns into the monstrous Mr. Hyde.

Novel — a very long story.

Plot — the main story of a book.

Social Studies — an area of study involving how people interact.

Index